THE EX RECOVERY BLUEPRINT

THE EX RECOVERY BLUEPRINT

Strategies to Win Back Your Ex

INNER POWER

Inner Strength Counselling

CONTENTS

1	Introduction	1
2	When Strong Relationships Go Sour	3
3	Sex Differences	6
4	Slow Down to Think	11
5	Reclaiming Confidence & Rekindle	17
6	Crafting A Fresh Relationship	23

CHAPTER 1

Introduction

Countless couples worldwide have parted ways with their ideal partners due to simple misunderstandings, which is truly disheartening. Many of these breakups could have been avoided had both partners understood each other's thoughts and desires within the relationship.

The reality is that men and women, being biologically distinct, unknowingly do things that can push their partners away instead of keeping them close. You might be feeling hurt or confused by the sudden end of your relationship. However, the truth is that even strong relationships often end needlessly.

Yes, needlessly. With a bit more understanding of how the opposite gender thinks, breakups could be prevented entirely. It's entirely possible to turn your past relationship into a lifelong, happy partnership where neither of you even thinks of seeking another partner.

If you've recently split from your true love, don't lose hope. There's still a chance to win them back, and it's simpler than you might imagine. Even if you've tried everything to express your desire to reunite, you might have noticed it's not working out as planned.

The problem lies in the fact that we're not taught how the opposite gender thinks, leaving it mostly a mystery to most people. We end up trying tactics that we believe might work without considering what our partner truly prefers.

This book offers straightforward tactics that can change your ex's perspective of you and reignite their love for you.

Are you ready to rekindle your relationship with your ex? Are you prepared for them to fall in love with you again, but this time, even deeper?

If so, let's delve into the valuable insights...

CHAPTER 2

When Strong Relationships Go Sour

How you handle a breakup greatly influences your strategy to win back your ex-partner. If the breakup involved crying, threats, violence, or dramatic scenes, it might have damaged your chances, but it's not an insurmountable hurdle. With determination, almost anything is possible.

Breakups usually don't happen out of the blue. If you're attentive to the relationship, you'll likely notice signs indicating a rift. Your partner might suddenly become busy, less communicative, or emotionally distant.

In response, it's natural to seek reassurance of their feelings, but pushing too hard often drives them further away—the "dance of death" in a relationship. Breaking this cycle is essential to avoiding a breakup. If you manage to pull back, your partner might be surprised by your change and begin pursuing you. Yet, controlling emotions in such moments can be challenging for most people, leading to actions they know they shouldn't take.

When your partner says, "We need to talk," it often signals bad news. This cue initiates the first phase of your plan to win back your ex. You need to act swiftly but calmly.

Avoid portraying the breakup as a major concern. No tears, no pleading. Refrain from behaviors that resemble begging; maintain your self-worth. This nonchalant demeanor can make a significant impact.

If you're afraid of that and think pleading will convey your feelings better, think again. Begging rarely changes their mind. Instead, a change in your approach—acting indifferent—can disrupt their expectations. By remaining composed and detached, you challenge their assumptions, leaving them disoriented. It requires effort, but it's a key step towards your ultimate goal of winning them back.

* * *

Unfortunately, even the strongest relationships sometimes take a turn for the worse, even though the reasons might not be immediately clear.

There are numerous factors behind why good relationships break down and result in a breakup. It could involve petty arguments or a sudden lack of communication from your ex, leaving you puzzled and disconnected.

When people are hurt and uncertain about their partner's stance in the relationship, they often end up doing the opposite of what could bring their ex back to them.

This happens because men and women tend to approach these situations based on what seems logical or appealing to their own gender. Understanding that men and women think differently is a crucial lesson. Using male logic to win back a female or vice versa usually backfires.

What's truly disheartening is that, despite their sincere intentions, both men and women tend to do things that repel the person they want to reconcile with. Without realizing it, they unknowingly push away their ex, going against what they should be doing to rebuild the relationship.

Many times, people find themselves unintentionally driving their ex further away instead of bringing them closer, without realizing their actions' consequences. Reflect on your current approach to winning back your ex – is it actually working or inadvertently pushing them farther away, worsening your feelings?

Let's explore the thoughts men and women often have during relationships and how they interpret their partner's actions. These insights can offer a deeper understanding of what might have gone wrong and provide guidance on how to navigate challenges when good relationships hit rough patches.

CHAPTER 3

Sex Differences

You might think it's obvious, but besides the evident differences, there are crucial hormonal and biological variations that distinguish men and women.

Consider this: when men aim to lower their stress, they often seek ways to increase testosterone. This might mean they watch the news after a long day, triggering their "fix it" mode. They may engage with others' problems because it fuels their desire to solve worldly issues, even if they appear motionless on the couch. During this time, they might not be available for immediate real-life problems as they focus on managing their stress levels.

Raised testosterone levels make men feel more positive and prompt them to address their own issues after winding down from a challenging workday where they've strived to demonstrate their role as providers to loved ones.

Contrarily, women have contrasting biological drives, which can pose challenges in relationships. When women experience increased testosterone levels, it can elevate stress, leading them to argue about seemingly trivial matters their partner may struggle to comprehend.

To reduce stress, women seek to boost oxytocin levels. Interestingly, oxytocin termed the "cuddle hormone" informally, is linked to maternal behavior and strengthens the desire to form stronger bonds with a partner.

For women to produce oxytocin, they require feelings of love, appreciation, and being cherished. If they sense their partner is distancing themselves, for any reason, it triggers a surge of testosterone, heightening stress levels and causing defensiveness.

Conversely, when a man's testosterone decreases, his stress levels rise, leading to a similar defensive reaction.

Fascinating?

THE IMPACT HORMONES HAVE ON RELATIONSHIPS

Consider the times when you've been in a fantastic mood, eagerly anticipating seeing your partner. Throughout the day, you might have engaged in activities that boosted your self-esteem. If you're a woman, chatting with friends about various matters might have helped ease your stress and increased your oxytocin levels, leaving you feeling amazing!

However, at the end of your partner's workday, he might be stressed and tense after a tough day. He might not feel inclined to discuss his problems as it triggers the wrong hormonal response in his system. His only desire might be to unwind—perhaps by catching up on world events in front of the TV for a bit.

But here's the catch: he's faced with a partner who wants to converse, share, cuddle, and be affectionate at a time when his stress levels are high, maybe even overwhelming. He hasn't had the chance to relax from his own stressful day, yet he's met with a partner who seems unperturbed and doesn't quite grasp his needs. This is a straightforward example, but can you see the issue here? Even the strongest relationships can suffer due to these basic hormonal differences between men and women if there's a lack of understanding about them.

Of course, there are relationships that encounter challenges for various other reasons.

OTHER STUFF IMPACT RELATIONSHIPS AS WELL

What occurs when you've seemingly done everything right, yet your ex still distances themselves from you?

There are moments in relationships when things go awry without any apparent reason. You might have felt everything was going smoothly, yet your ex abruptly stopped contacting you, ceased returning messages, and completely withdrew from the relationship as if you weren't part of it.

The person who feels rejected often believes they haven't done anything to cause this, but the partner who pulled away may have had different expectations about the relationship's direction from the start.

When individuals fall in love, they release a hormone similar to the one found in people with Obsessive-Compulsive Disorder (OCD). This hormone often leads people in love to obsess over their partners, impacting their appetite, sleep, and focus at work.

However, feeling this way doesn't guarantee your partner felt the same intensity simultaneously. Just as not everyone gets hungry at the same time, people don't experience identical feelings simultaneously.

The issue arises when one person in the relationship starts contemplating its future, imagining various scenarios beyond the dating phase. They might assume the relationship has deepened significantly, while the other person may still be figuring out their emotions. This disparity is sometimes termed the 'instant relationship,' where one partner believes they're dating while the other feels the relationship has progressed further without mutual understanding.

A common mistake in such situations is attempting to persuade the partner to stay or professing an overwhelming amount of love. When men witness this behavior in women, they might feel compelled to slow down or even break away, perceiving their partner as needy and desperate, which can be a turn-off.

Conversely, some men commit the same error as the women they adore. They may try to convince her that he loves her more than anyone else and is better suited for her than anyone else. However, they often fail to comprehend what they're doing wrong in these scenarios.

CHAPTER 4

Slow Down to Think

THINK ABOUT WHAT DREW YOU TOGETHER IN THE BEGINNING

In nearly every breakup, the key to winning your ex back often traces back to the initial phase of your relationship.

Recall the early days when you first met your partner. Reflect on your demeanor and theirs during that time. It's likely you both exhibited your best selves, making concerted efforts to ensure the other person had a great time. Any minor quirks in behavior or personality might have been overlooked because you were driven to make a favorable impression.

Now, contrast that with your recent interactions with your ex. Were you both enjoying each other's company or caught up in arguments, stress, distress, or worries about each other's thoughts?

If the latter was more common, chances are your ex's current perception of you might revolve around moments of conflict, anger, tears, distress, and concern about the relationship's future. This doesn't foster positive thoughts about a happy future together. Instead, they might be contemplating finding someone more reminiscent of the person they were when they first met.

Indeed, the person your ex fell in love with initially was the upbeat, confident, positive, driven, and self-assured individual you portrayed. You likely made them feel joyous when together, and they cherished the anticipation of seeing you amidst your busy schedule.

So, what changed?

MISTAKES MADE

Have you found yourself trying to convince your ex to reunite with you post-breakup, believing they're the one you're destined to spend your life with? However, have you considered whether your ex shares these sentiments?

If you've been persistently reaching out to your ex via calls, texts, emails, or messages, attempting to persuade them of your compatibility, you might inadvertently be pushing them farther away. These continuous efforts often come across as desperation, a quality neither men nor women find appealing. Desperation exudes insecurity and clinginess, traits that are generally unattractive.

Confidence, on the other hand, is universally appealing. Both men and women are drawn to individuals who display self-assurance, know their desires, and don't rely on someone else for their happiness.

However, someone who suddenly believes their sole source of happiness is tethered to you becomes less appealing. Your partner likely fell for the happy, self-assured version of you, not the miserable, desperate one they're witnessing now. They might wonder what happened to the person they initially fell in love with because the current unhappy version doesn't evoke the same feelings.

Imagine spending time with someone who's consistently miserable, arguing, pleading, and attempting to persuade you whenever you're around them. It wouldn't be enjoyable, right? You'd probably seek out more enjoyable company instead.

So, if you've fallen into the trap of pleading or begging your ex to return, driving them further away, there might still be hope to mend your relationship. Even if you've been constantly messaging or calling, there are ways to potentially salvage the situation.

CONTROL THE URGE

If you're aiming to bring your ex back into your life, your initial step is to refrain from contacting them in any form. Cease texting, calling, or emailing. Avoid seeking information about them through mutual friends—just stop.

Recall who you were before the relationship. You likely had a life of your own: a job, friends, and hobbies. Revisit those aspects and revive them as they were before your ex entered your life.

Even though you might not feel up to it, resist the urge to sit at home waiting for communication. Instead, put on a smile and spend time with supportive family and friends. Surround yourself with people who uplift your spirits and avoid those who bring negativity or exacerbate your feelings about the breakup. These individuals won't aid in your efforts to rekindle the relationship.

The key is to rediscover the happy, independent version of yourself that your ex was initially drawn to.

After some time of silence, your ex may start to wonder why you haven't reached out. They might begin to worry about you. While you're not there yet, this marks a good beginning. Consider this: your ex worrying implies that there's still a level of care for you.

The significant lesson here is to halt contact and focus on your personal growth and well-being.

***

In short, during a breakup, the urge to know what your ex is doing or to contact them can be overwhelming. However, certain actions can inadvertently push your ex further away. Here are some behaviors to avoid:

Blow up their phone: Continuously calling your ex, especially after an unsuccessful conversation, can be seen as harassment. Avoid repeatedly dialing their number, leaving multiple messages, or waiting for them to return your calls. It only intensifies the situation and may lead to unwanted consequences.

Passing by Their Residence: Obsessively driving by your ex's place only adds unnecessary stress. Constantly checking if their car is there or seeking signs of their activities is counterproductive. It wastes time, fuels unnecessary worry, and might make them feel uncomfortable or threatened.

Contacting Their Social Circle: Attempting to involve their family or friends in your relationship issues is unwise. Using them as intermediaries or speaking negatively about your ex will likely backfire. It may strain relationships and make your ex resentful.

Sending Them Stuff: While gestures of affection seem kind, bombarding your ex with gifts won't necessarily win them back. Gifts won't resolve underlying issues or magically reignite the relationship.

Stalking Their Social Media: Constantly monitoring your ex's online presence, stalking their social media, or creating fake profiles to spy on them is unhealthy. It prevents both of you from moving on and damages the chances of reconciliation.

Making Suicide Threats: Using threats of self-harm as a means to garner sympathy or attention is never appropriate. It's a serious matter that requires professional help, not manipulation in a relationship.

Dating for Revenge: Involving yourself romantically with their friends or family out of spite will only complicate matters. It's unfair to drag innocent parties into your relationship issues.

Instantly Reply if They Reach Out: If your ex initiates contact, resist the urge to immediately respond or rush back to them. Take your time to consider their intentions and avoid becoming too emotionally invested too quickly.

Remember, resorting to violence or engaging in destructive behavior only damages your chances of reconciliation and can have serious legal repercussions. The goal is to resolve matters amicably, not escalate them.

CHAPTER 5

Reclaiming Confidence & Rekindle

RECLAIMING YOUR CONFIDENCE AND JOY

Movies often paint unrealistic fairy-tale images of love, making us believe that after intense drama, conflicts, and arguments, our true love will magically come to their senses, and we'll live happily ever after. However, this idealistic portrayal is more fantasy than reality.

The truth is, your ex isn't the sole source of your happiness. You are the holder of the key to your own happiness. You don't require another person in your life to find fulfillment. All you truly need are your own interests, hobbies, passions, and activities that bring you joy.

Recall the time when you first met your ex, chances are, you were already content, self-reliant, and confident. These qualities are incredibly attractive to others. So, take some time to enjoy life. Hang out with friends, and watch lighthearted comedy movies that won't remind you of your ex or make you feel upset. Treat yourself to a new outfit or haircut. Dedicate some time to exercise and take care of yourself.

When you look good, you feel good, and that radiates attractiveness to everyone around you. As your confidence returns, you'll start noticing positivity in various aspects of your life.

This approach serves another purpose too. Not only will it aid in moving past the breakup, but it will also reconnect you with the person you were when your ex fell in love with you.

RECONNECT STRATEGICALLY

Once you've rebuilt your confidence, you'll start feeling better about yourself, like you did before you met your ex. This also puts you in a good spot if you want to see your ex again.

Sometimes, if you stop reaching out, your ex might get concerned and call you to check-in. If they do, it means they care in some way. But don't rush into the meeting too soon. It's essential to ensure you feel more like your cheerful self first.

If your ex hasn't reached out and you've worked on boosting your confidence for a couple of weeks, you might consider a friendly phone call just to say 'hi'. Don't push to discuss the relationship or ask them to meet up for coffee. Simply let them know you wanted to say hello. It's a chance to share what you've been up to since the breakup, like going out and enjoying yourself.

It's okay to casually mention that you've thought about them sometimes, but keep the conversation light and don't dive into relationship talks immediately. This is crucial.

Before ending the conversation, it's nice to mention catching up at some point but don't set a specific time or place.

PLAY IT SMART

Men often enjoy chasing something they believe they can't easily have. However, some women take this to an extreme by dating someone new just to make their ex jealous. But this tactic rarely works. Jumping into a new relationship immediately may give the impression that your past relationship wasn't significant to you and that you've moved on. Even if your ex still has feelings for you, they might not act on them.

The concept of playing hard to get involves not dropping everything and rushing to respond the moment your ex reaches out. Instead, let their call go to voicemail and return it when you're feeling positive and happy.

If they propose a date, agree but suggest a different day. For instance, if they want to meet for coffee on a Friday, agree but mention that Saturday would suit you better. Regardless of what you have planned for the day, convey that you're occupied with your life. If they want to be part of it again, they'll need to put in some effort to catch your attention.

Here are some conversational topics to avoid during the date with your ex:

1. Asking if they're currently dating someone.
2. Inquiring if they miss you.
3. Suggesting a rekindling of the relationship.

It's crucial to refrain from initiating these discussions. Remember, your ex chose to end things, likely due to feeling suffocated by neediness. To avoid coming off as needy, steer clear of such topics and any hints that imply you've been eagerly waiting for their return. Resist the urge to disclose that you haven't dated anyone else, but also refrain from inventing stories about multiple new relationships. Confidence is key during this meeting, even if it's a trait you've never possessed before. If you're lacking in confidence, the next chapter offers guidance on how to cultivate it before this crucial encounter. Above all, don't let your ex's presence shake the confidence you've built within yourself.

During your reunion, schedule another meeting in advance to limit your time together. Let them know you have a specific time you must leave. This might cut your conversation short, but it'll likely leave them wanting more of your company.

After your first meeting, resist the urge to immediately arrange another date. Give it a few days and see if they initiate contact first.

Remember, your ex still remembers the reasons for the breakup. One meeting won't erase those issues. If you truly want them back, you'll need to spend time rekindling their feelings for you.

However, be cautious with the 'hard to get' approach. You don't want to become someone unappealing. These are individuals who cross the line from confidence to arrogance. They assert strong opinions, even if they lead to arguments, and they refuse to accept any responsibility for the relationship's end, blaming their ex entirely.

If negative thoughts arise during your time with your ex, be ready to end the date and leave while things are still positive. Failing to do so might risk losing them for good.

REKINDLING THE LOVE

Consider this: your ex was initially drawn to you due to a level of attraction. As you spent time together, those feelings likely grew. However, something went wrong, leading to the relationship's end. They might claim their feelings have changed or simply vanish, ignoring your attempts at contact.

Even though the initial flame may have dimmed, there's still a spark lingering in their thoughts. Your task is to reignite that spark and rekindle the connection. If you're serious about winning them back, discussing what went wrong is necessary, but timing is crucial—don't rush into it.

Following a breakup, both parties need time to reflect and process. When you eventually meet your ex after some time apart, refrain from bringing up the breakup during that first encounter. Instead, show them the happy, confident person they fell for initially.

Some might wonder why you haven't pursued them or demanded explanations. This curiosity might prompt them to reach out for another meeting, just to see your next move.

However, there are others who may interpret your actions as a mind game, keeping their distance. If your ex falls into this category, wait a week after your first meeting, then reach out for a friendly catch-up.

While these strategies seem straightforward, their purpose is to make your ex think of you when you're not around. The more they contemplate you in your absence, the higher the chance they'll want to reconnect.

CHAPTER 6

Crafting A Fresh Relationship

Longing for the past won't bring back your old relationship. That chapter has closed, and instead of fixing a broken relationship, the aim is to forge a new, stronger one.

Consider the aspects you cherished in your previous relationship and weigh them against the ones causing issues. Selectively choose what to carry forward and what to leave behind.

Once you've reconnected and started dating your ex regularly, it's time to address the past. If they're hesitant to talk, don't push. Playing 'hard to get' in the right way encourages them to seek your attention, paving the way for a more opportune moment to discuss past issues.

Rather than dwelling on what went wrong, inquire about what improvements they'd like to see. This empowers them to brainstorm solutions, fostering a positive approach to strengthening your bond and turning it into a collaborative and enjoyable experience.

Focusing on past problems or negativity risks steering conversations toward a downward spiral. Avoid this by centering discussions on positive actions both of you can take.

With a clearer vision of the new relationship's desires, rebuilding it on a solid foundation becomes much more attainable.

DATING VS. REBUILDING A RELATIONSHIP

It's common to assume that dating your ex means you're back in a relationship, but that might not be their perspective. Dating merely entails spending time together, and enjoying activities, without defining the relationship yet.

Avoid assuming their thoughts or pressuring them for reconciliation timelines; this can convey desperation and push them further. Instead, focus on enjoying each other's company and having fun. Maintain your independence and avoid dropping everything for them.

While rekindling the relationship might be your goal, prioritize your personal life too. Your friends, family, work, and hobbies shape your identity outside the relationship, bolstering your confidence and reducing stress.

Occasionally, express unavailability for a date, demonstrating that your life doesn't revolve solely around them. This creates a dynamic where they pursue you, gradually prompting them to broach the topic of reconciling the relationship.

EMBRACING AUTHENTICITY

Once you've succeeded in reuniting with your ex, it's vital not to conceal your true self. Sometimes, individuals adopt certain behaviors or phrases to entice others, but this façade isn't genuine. If you're not authentic, who is your partner truly falling for? And how will they react when the real you emerge after the act?

If your goal is to genuinely rebuild the relationship, avoid resorting to tricks, mind games, or manipulative tactics to win their affection. Embrace your authentic self—the confident, playful, and enjoyable individual they were drawn to in the first place.

Strive to be the best version of yourself: maintain a positive outlook, seek joy in life, indulge in hobbies, cherish time with friends, and prioritize self-care. When you look and feel great, your confidence radiates.

Ultimately, your ex fell for the person you were at the start. There's a good chance they'll still cherish you for who you truly are. Offer them the best version of yourself—a version that captures their heart once more.

Wish you the best.

www.ingramcontent.com/pod-product-compliance
Lightning Source LLC
Chambersburg PA
CBHW071326080526
44587CB00018B/3354